Después de ese Tan Largo

empezamos: Con una Serie de Sugerencias con las que Creemos que podemos SER mejores y dejar de Perder el tiempo con Situaciones de Agresividad, Intolerancia, Racismo e Ignorancia

Capítulo Uno Los Problemas se presentan con Su Respectiva Solución

Capítulo Dos A Reserva de Su Mejor Opinión **AQUÍ** Empezamos:

Capítulo Tres Que Pasa CON los que como DICEN que "Ya Graduaron" de High School

Capítulo Cuatro Que Debemos Saber, Entender y Hacer para que **regresen** "Los trabajos"

Capítulo Cinco Volviendo a Relacionar con Los TRABAJOS a Nuestros Egresados de "High School, Universidades y Doctorados.

Capítulo Seis En Estados Unidos se habla POCO de Devaluaciones PERO si le Preguntamos a quien Hace Las Compras en Casa Va a Opinar **MUY** Distinto.

Capítulo Siete Aquí Enumeraremos de manera Más Generalizada **Las Conclusiones** de los

Temas Anteriores para que Vayan Tomando una Forma Final.

Capítulo Ocho
La BARDA Fronteriza No es Una Buena Solución "MEJOR" que SEA Una Franja de Progreso y Cordialidad

Capítulo Nueve
Para este Plan, aquí Van Estas Otras Sugerencias.

Capítulo Diez
Otra Importante Sugerencia Sería Implementar Centros de Capacitación para To2 los Niveles de ESTE Personal.

Capítulo Once
"Si Se Pude" Convertir Algo FEO en Algo BONITO y Progresista Refiriéndonos a "La Barda o Muro Divisorio" de Las Fronteras con Estados Unidos

Donald Trump

ya GANO

ahora a esperar que "Regresen los Trabajos"

Opiniones Sugerencias y Pedi2 al correo: <u>libroscortitos@yahoo.com</u>

Escritos Cortitos **PERO** que Dicen Mucho
en Su Serie

¿Realidades o Novelas?

Contáctanos en:

TWITTER   @Libros Cortitos   o

FACEBOOK   LaReforma Migratoria

en FACEBOOK   Realodades ONovelas

o en Nuestra

Página Web   realidadesonovelas.webs.com

o Para Sugerencias de Temas, Comentarios y Peticiones (Como en la Radio):
holasoyjavy@yahoo.com

Queda totalmente prohibido so pena de enfrentarse a las consecuencias legales de las leyes en vigor, hacer o usar cualquier reproducción ya sea total o parcial del contenido de este libro así como el uso de cualquiera de sus partes con fines comerciales aún estando editado, modificado o alterado de alguna forma en uso Impreso o Digital en todas sus Modalidades sin la aprobación por escrito del autor principal.

Por: Javy JG

Made in the USA
Coppell, TX
03 December 2024

41663387R00036

RAGINI MICHAELS

Discover The Secrets To Raising The Perfect Schnoodle

Become Your Schnoodle's Best Friend & Create A Lifelong Bond

First edition

This book was professionally typeset on Reedsy.
Find out more at reedsy.com

The author dedicates this book to the power of Love, in all its forms, and expresses gratitude to the poet, Hafiz, who inspired the name of my belovedschnoodle.

'Be the person your dog thinks you are!'

J.W. Stephen

Contents

Preface

If you're looking for love, a dog will happily provide it. The trick is for you to receive it. My schnoodle, Hafiz, was my best teacher, showing me exactly what needed to be done to reach this amazing place of unconditional giving. Believe me, only love could entice me to consider the needs of others to the degree that my entire life revolved around it.

I'm not saying you can't find this love in lots of places. But for me? This adorable ball of fur granted me the real secret of love. It happened the day my needs and desires became second to his. I am grateful for our fabulous 15 years together, including all the multiple difficulties and delights.

Life remains a mystery, but now it's a journey filled with love and gratitude, especially when I remember that true joy rests just on the other side of my own needs and desires.

Much Love,
Ragini

Introduction

Welcome to *Discover The Secrets To Raising The Perfect Schnoodle: Become Your Schnoodle's Best Friend And Create A Lifelong Bond.* I spent 15 years with my precious little schnoodle, named Hafiz (after the Sufi poet). It was one of the most amazing journeys of my life. Despite my endeavors in personal growth, meditation, and spiritual inquiry, I didn't expect to find what I was looking for with a dog. But I did. And I will be forever grateful.

I've decided to not only share the details of how I learned to best care for this delightful but demanding little fellow, but how his presence and very being opened my heart to a completely unique experience of love I had not previously encountered.

My 15 years with this little bundle of joy, as demanding and as difficult as he was, gave me the gift I had been seeking. I honestly had a taste of true love for the first time. The circumstances that led to this include the fact that I had never married and had no children. So, to be honest, I was a novice at putting myself second and someone else first.

This darling little bundle of fur became my highest priority and the focal point of my everyday life. Everything simply revolved around him and his needs. Not because I always wanted to. But because his undeniable beauty and love of life had captured my heart. I just wanted to be sure he was happy - top priority. Drove my friends crazy and turned my professional life topsy-turvy. But I was helpless to do anything other than make certain he was happy, healthy, and enjoying the life he was now sharing with me.

If you're in the market for a schnoodle, I want to share what I learned. This urge rests only in the joy I experienced from living with such an adorable being and learning how to become his, and my own, best friend.

|

What A Schnoodle Owner Needs To Know
If you know nothing about being a responsible pet owner, I'd like to share how I moved from feeling terrified with this little 8-week-old ball of fluff that easily fit into my hand to loving him so much that his needs were always my first consideration. It was a radical shift to care about another that much. But in fact, it felt great! Who knew an adorable fluff ball would be the answer to all my questions

about love and relationships.

So here goes. I absolutely wanted a designer dog. I knew it would make me feel uniquely special. But first, I needed to know exactly what a designer dog was. Thus, the research began, which is what I'm sharing in this little book.

INTRODUCTION

Compliments of Pixabay.com

The Pros and Cons Of A Designer Dog

I discovered designer dogs are hybrids. A schnoodle is a hybrid resulting from crossbreeding between a purebred schnauzer and a purebred poodle. Both breeds are naturally hypoallergenic. They do shed some, but very little compared to other breeds.

The schnauzer breed usually has a streak of stubbornness, and the poodle usually shows high intelligence. These combined traits created a challenging but delightful and charming personality.

Whatever else you may feel about designer dogs, they are incredibly adorable! The schnoodle has soft fur, offers little shedding, and is very smart! They do come in 3 sizes, like poodles. Hafiz was small, but only in stature. His way of meeting the world telegraphed strength, courage, and the energy of an explorer - as well as being true to the schnoodle promise of being adorable - all traits I enjoyed every day.

The downside? Designer dogs are usually very expensive. So, take the time to check out whether the puppies are being raised by people running puppy farms or genuine breeders.

Do your homework and make sure the breeder is reputable

and treats their dogs well, with both love and respect. Check out their credentials and specifically how they run their business.

Often people ask about the difference between a so-called mutt and a designer dog. There is an answer to this. Usually, a mutt results from parents of different breeds who do not have any credentials (not purebred) with no intention of creating a new breed. If you're interested in this debate over whether designer dogs are just mutts, you can Google the controversy for more information, or check out https://www.nation algeographic.com/premium/article/mixed-breed-mutt-designer-dogs

Why Owners Believe Designer Dogs Are Worth The Expense

Most owners will agree that the adorable factor and potential non- hypoallergenic factor make the high cost of these cute puppies worth- while. People in America highly value having both an adorable dog and minimized shedding. And, because they're expensive, they also denote some obvious disposable income, also highly valued in America.

Now let's explore the 10 ways you can become your schnoodle's best friend. It's true that people say dogs are man's best friend. And they certainly fill that expectation. But I found that friendship happens best when you become their best friend first.

2

Establishing Your Alpha Status

I imagine you already know that dogs relate to being in a pack. And a pack always has a leader. In your case, you automatically become the leader of the pack, even though you may only be two. If you

don't claim the alpha position, you're in for trouble. Because I was not an alpha female, the first year of our relationship was a constant battle. I was advised that because Hafiz was male, he would naturally be more headstrong and less accommodating than most females. He was, in fact, quite adamant about getting his way and doing what he wanted, regardless of my input.

I learned that without my claiming the alpha status, we would 1) always be in a fight, and 2) he would remain unsure and nervous about the territory and how to navigate it successfully. That nervousness and uncertainty generated more anxiety and more behaviors that were less than fun or acceptable.

At first, I thought claiming alpha status meant asserting my will over his. An ugly approach that didn't work well for us at all. In fact, it only made matters much worse. Then I discovered a life-saving perspective.

What if I could establish my place in his life as a human being, rather than another dog in competition for being head of the pack? Could I just be the human who consistently gave him food, played with him, and kept him safe and feeling secure? That's when I ran into the two basic competing views of dog training.

Dominance Training vs. Positive Reinforcement Training

Dominance training has its roots in the study of wolves skewed by the tactics and methods used in the military. Apparently, dominance tactics do work. But they were not for me, and I certainly didn't want to have that kind of relationship with my sweet little puppy. However, I needed to be the one who called the shots and got listened to. Thankfully, I then ran into Positive-Reinforcement training.

Ah! This was fantastic! Give the dog a treat when they do what you want. Period!

Practice it over and over until he gets that every time he does the desired behavior, he gets rewarded! Simple! And it worked! Always stay calm and ignore the unwanted behavior when it appears. Then guide the pooch to the desired behavior with the promise of a treat when performed. Voila!

9

Easy Peasy!

If you learn how to do this early on, you will fill your life journey with your pet with more fun, more joy, and a lot more love and affection flowing both ways. I also discovered that my little schnoodle wanted to please me. (Or maybe he just wanted that treat.) Regardless, the positive-reinforcement training laid the groundwork for a happier and more fun-filled connection every day.

Compliments of Pixabay.com

3

Make Training Into Concentrated Play

S chnoodles love to play and have fun. But the key to a happy living arrangement is for the dog to do what you need him to do when you need it done. Thus, setting aside the time to practice

is a necessity. But remember, 10 to 15 minutes a day of concentratedtraining is more than enough.

Practicing commands is a true bottom-line necessity! *Sit. Stay. Wait. Come. Down. OK* (that means the dog can move or is released from the command). Some others are: *Drop it* (hold out your hand under the toy he has in his mouth and when he does it, give the reward). Or you could say, *Give it!* Just be consistent in what you're teaching him to respond to.

Sit. Stay. Wait. Come. Down. OK.

There are the 6 basic commands your pooch needs to not only know but respond to whenever he hears you say them.

Honestly, these basic commands could save his life, so don't think this is silly or just for your convenience.

As a dog owner, it is your responsibility to train your pet with, at minimum, these commands. And you succeed by practicing them every day, over and over. It may seem boring to you but think of your dog. So, make sure he is happy when training him. The way to do that is to make certain he receives:

1. a treat (a healthy one) every time he responds properly to the commands,

2. a happy and congratulating comment from you with the proper voice and facial expressions of joy and delight

3. a pat on the head (or some kind of kinesthetic or touch reward as well

One Caveat: When engaged in your time for training, be sure you keep your dog's attention focused on you. They can often get easily distracted, so pay attention to bringing their attention back to you during training time.

Hafiz Being Distracted During Training Time

4

Letting Playtime Be Just Play

Training is hard work, for you and for your dog. So, when it's time to just play, be sure that is all you do. No training per se. Just easy fun with lots of running or movement of any kind.

- Play fetch! Throw the toy and let him run and get it and bring itback to you. Have fun. Be excited with him through the throw andall the way through his getting to it and bringing it back to you.

- Play Catch Me If You Can. Let the dog chase you or you chase thedog, pretending as if you have something he wants, or you want.Or make it an actual toy you keep with you as you run around, orlet the dog run with the toy while you engage in chasing after itand getting it from him.

- Play Tug-Of-War with a rope or toy that allows both you and the dog to engage in pulling, trying to get the toy from the other.

- Give the dog his favorite chew toy but stay engaged, if only to just keep a connection going. (Taste good? Like that? Feel good? It smells good?)

- Play Hide & Seek. Hide your dog's favorite toy and then tell him to go find it. Keep encouraging him to look everywhere until he finds it and brings it back to you.

- Go from room to room in your house and call out his name. When he comes, give him a treat. Then go to another room and call out his name. Keep going until you've hit all the rooms.

- Teach him a new trick.

- Take the puppy for a long walk through a place he hasn't been before

- Give him puzzle games and stay engaged while he's figuring it out, giving congratulations every time he figures out a part of the puzzle.

There are so many things you can do to just play.

But the main thing here is to do them together.

Continue to give your pooch the praise and touch he adores. A pat on the head, a congratulatory word. He just wants your attention and presence, so be sure to give it to him. Make his playtime, your playtime *with* him. That builds and strengthens your connection and your emerging friendship.

Hafiz and Friend In Their Favorite Game

5

Providing Mental Stimulation With Toys & Without

Dogs are much smarter than you may think - especially schnoodles! So that means your pooch NEEDS mental stimulation.

So, what are your dog's mental traits? Curiosity, of course. And memory? They might remember better than you! And schnoodles love to solve problems! These are just a few. You might take your dog on a challenging walk because you know it's good for their body to do physically challenging things. Likewise, exercise your dog's mind because it's good for their brain.

The biggest issue is that if you don't keep your schnoodle mentally stimulated, the dog will get bored. And when a dog is bored, they do things to entertain themselves that you won't like - like tearing up pillows, getting into food that doesn't belong to them, digging up dirt in the yard and then carrying it into the house, and on and on. So, games are essential if you want to avoid the shenanigans of bored dogs!

Puzzle games, food puzzle games, strangely shaped objects filled with treats that are tough to get out. There are literally hundreds of these types of games on Amazon and other places. And these brain teaser games improve your dog's sleep and disposition

Compliments of Pixabay.com

Teaching A New Dog Old Tricks

One of the most enjoyable things to do is to teach your schnoodle some

tricks. Learning tricks requires a lot of concentration, thus giving his brain (and probably yours) a good workout! Here are a few to try out:

- Shake (meaning give me your paw)
- Roll Over
- Lay Down
- Cover Your Eyes
- Cross Your Front Legs

I never taught Hafiz to beg because I didn't like the notion of him ever having to beg for anything. But it is certainly a standard trick that isnot too difficult to teach.

Of course, you use treats when teaching your dog a trick. Do you remember positive reinforcement conditioning from earlier? Positive reinforcement works beautifully.

A Few Tips: Don't *talk* your dog through a new trick. Watch him and when he performs what you want him to do (like lifting his paw into the air), praise him immediately for performing the trick (give it a name) and then offer him a treat. This is a much easier and more rewarding way to teach a trick than trying to get the puppy to do something that he is not doing spontaneously in the moment.

6

Committing To 'Rinse & Repeat' Daily

Without embracing the power of this lesson, your friendship with your schnoodle will not be solid and secure! As with all things, success rests in the hands of commitment. If you want the outcome of a happy relationship with your schnoodle, you must embrace the fact that results rest in your hands.

At some point, most of us realize we achieve learning through the simple act of repeating information until it becomes our own knowledge. The same goes for your puppy. Consistent repetition lays down new neural pathways in the brain for your schnoodle and for you. This creates the pattern you know as a simple stimulus response conditioning (remember Pavlov's dogs?).

There are several basic reasons that training with your dog is NEVER over. The main reason is that things don't stay the same:

- Like you, your schnoodle will keep aging.
- Your environment can change.
- Your habits can change.
- Your lifestyle can change.
- Your dog's personality or temperament can change.

These shifts predicate learning new environments, new habits, and often how to live with new and never-ending body aches, pains, or injuries.

Hafiz Resting Outside During Training Time

When You Need To Correct Your Schnoodle

Professional dog trainer Ed Frawley in an article published in Leer-burg.com spoke to the common notion that punishing your dog is the best way to correct unacceptable behavior. He suggests that when correcting your dog, it works best to keep the goal as positive, clear,and simple as possible.

So that means the outcome you're going for is simply to *change* your dog's behavior to a better or more acceptable response. The purpose is not to punish him to prevent a repeat offense. That doesn't identify the desired change in behavior.

This takes us back to the earlier chapter on how you positioned yourself as the alpha dog - through dominance or positive reinforcement conditioning. Finding what works best for you and for your puppy reinforces your emerging friendship and trust in your dependable guidance.

7

Gathering The Right Treats & Meals

Treats are a dog-owner's lifesaver. Dogs like food! And treats are also an instantaneous reward. Treats are perfect for easily getting great training results that are repeatable on-cue. Here's what to pay attention to:

- The dog must love the treat. The more he loves the treat, the more likely he will happily perform to get it.
- Every time you give a treat to reward a desired behavior, be sure to combine it with your voice and your touch. For example: patting his head while saying 'Great job, little schnoodle darling!!!'
- When your pup performs the desired behavior, provide the treat immediately. So, keep them in your pocket, and when training, always right in your hand, ready to be delivered!

The best kinds of treats have a tasty flavor, a pleasant smell, and balanced nutrition.. You want their size to be small enough to be chewed quickly and easily, and many prefer those treats that are free of additives and don't interfere with the pup's dietary needs. I always like those that were easy to break up so I could make sure I wasn't feeding him too much.

If your dog has any allergies (which many dogs do), check out the ingredients before buying the newest treat on the market.

What's the main point? Buy treats that are packed with non-allergicprotein, low in fillers, small, and tasty according to your puppy!

How Many Treats Are Too Many In A Day?

This is important. Know what your dog's dietary limit is for one day. The rule of thumb seems to be that no more than 10% of their food should be in treats. Really pay attention to this, please. It breaks my heart to see overweight dogs. It's unconscionable and uncaring to let this happen. So don't do it.

Give your puppy the recommended amount of food ONLY and take him on lots and lots of walks where he can run around, play, and use up those calories!

The Importance Of The Right Meals

There are so many opinions on this that I say it's best to do
2 things: talk to your vet and pay attention to your dog's
feedback. He likes it or he doesn't like it. He eats it or leaves
it untouched. There are lots of experts who say mixing up
their food is the best way to go. One brand here and another
brand there. Others say stick to one brand and that's it. No
changes. However, be alert to allergies or digestive issues
emerging. These can dictate what brands are the best
specifically for that allergy or digestive issue. Check with
your vet.

FooToppers

Whichever you decide to do, it's also good to know about
what's called *food toppers*. Food toppers are as the name
suggests. Toppers are things you put on top of your dog's food.
They can add variety to the diet and help with digestive issues.
Here are some of the most common ones, especially for picky
eaters:

- Canned Pumpkin

- A Raw Egg

- Cucumbers

- Bone Broth

- Plain Yogurt

- Blueberries

- Fresh Vegetables

- Sardines

Whatever you choose to feed your dog, please remember that it is one of the most important decisions you must make about caring for your dog with love and consideration for their needs. Sometimes just changing the food you've been giving your little one can heal an illness, shift a temperament issue, or increase their energy and mood in a single day.

Hafiz Showing His Adorable Puppy Face Asking, "Where Is My Treat?"

8

Resting & Relaxing Together

An important aspect of becoming your schnoodle's best friend is taking the time to both rest and relax together. When it's time for you to sit down and take a breather, invite your pooch

to jump up on your lap. (If you have a bigger guy, at least invite him to lie down next to your chair where you can reach his head to give him a pat or two.)

Resting for even a moment or two is a great time to reconnect and let your little guy know you haven't forgotten him. That makes him feel seen and safe. Never forget that your dog has great instincts, and he can sense when you are no longer with him, even if you're sitting right there.

The more you reach out to stay connected with your Schnoodle, the better. Verbal connection and physical touch are the best ways to let him know you're there, even if you're about to fall asleep in your chair.

Hafiz Catching A Nap On The Back Of His (And My) Favorite Chair

Reading, Meditating, Watching TV

These are 3 significant activities that practically shout out for the importance of connection time with your animal. All 3 of these activities demand your focused attention on something *other* than your best friend

- the tv show, the book you're reading, or attending to your inner world of thoughts and feelings. Don't sit there for even an hour without reconnecting with your dog.

What makes a connection? Once again, a simple verbal

30

recognition directed to your pooch, a physical pat on the head or a stroke of his body, or even getting up and bending over to whisper a sweet loving comment into his eyes while stroking his head or shoulder.

Remember. You are your dog's world. You are the alpha, the leader, the protector, the guide, not to mention his prime source of that wonderfulstuff called food.

You want a dog that is your best friend. Easy to make happen when you become and remain consistent with being his best friend too.

Sleeping Together

For some dogs, sleeping in your bed is just to be near you and to feel safe. For others, it is a matter of who's the boss. Here's a brief story.

Hafiz loved my bed. He wanted to sleep there from the very beginning. It took several months for me to get him to stop taking over my bed. He not only wanted to sleep in my bed, he wanted to dominate it. Howdid I know that?

He started the game by just climbing up on the bed and resting at the foot end. Then slowly, over a few days, he began moving up the bed until he finally got to the pillows where he settled down to sleep - and would not move.

when I came into the room, he would NOT get offthe pillows. He would growl at me. Then bark. And eventually I had to push him off the bed with big pillows. I used them so I wouldn't get hurt in case he moved on to biting me. He clearly believed those pillows were now completely his and not mine.

This was definitely not only a problem, but it was also the last straw! That event gave me the energy to go for claiming my alpha status (using the positive-reinforcement model, of course). And I did. And once we resolved that confusion, we never had to have an ugly pillow fight again. Life with Hafiz suddenly got a lot easier and much more fun.

9

Playing With Other Dogs
(Socialization #1)

It's important to keep introducing your puppy to other dogs. Without this experience, your adolescent or adult dog will most likely be uncomfortable in the presence of other animals. This means you'll be limiting yourself in the future when you want to enroll him in a doggie day care or have him stay overnight while you're on a trip.

Without these experiences, you might find your pooch being expelled from a doggie day care for unacceptable behavior. It won't be because he is a bad dog. Most likely it will be because he didn't learn how to be comfortable in a wide-range of different experiences.

You can easily jump into this socialization process by taking your dog to a dog park and letting him play with the other dogs. You could also sign him up to be part of a dog play group. And if that's too much socializing for you, just take him on daily walks where he can at least see other dogs, even if he doesn't get to interact.

The big outcome of this effort is that your dog is learning how to behave like a dog around other dogs. Keeping him away from these experiences will most likely produce behavior issues in the future .

Exposing your puppy to a wide range of varying experiences (sightsand sounds) teaches him what it feels like to be comfortable aroundunfamiliar sights, smells, and sounds. That means he'll be happier whenhe's around the unfamiliar and you'll be happier because your pooch isat ease and not attacking other dogs or quivering behind your legs infull fear.

Compliments of Pixabay.com

10

Playing With Other People
(Socialization#2)

You're naturally going to be highly protective of your new puppy. But here's the thing. You don't want to hide away your adorable, cuddly little schnoodle. And here's why.

You not only need your dog to know how to behave around other dogs. You also need your dog to know how to behave around other people. This means exposing your dog to social situations that include other people.

Designer dogs are so cuddly (especially schnoodles), your friends and others will naturally want to reach out and pet him. They will also use their voice to communicate friendliness when they say "Ohhh! How cute!" with a slightly higher pitch than we usually use with strangers on the street. And they also may move toward the puppy in rapturous joy at his cuteness. That means fast, unexpected movements, including quick arm movements coming toward your dog to pet him.

Letting your dog get used to these things is important. Keep an eye out for the overly zealous and intervene, for sure. Feel totally ok about asking that type of person to back off or slow down, or even cut them off completely. You don't want to give your dog an anxiety attack. But you do want to expose him to those things that could potentially give him one.

But also, keep an eye out for those who are also showing respect and awareness of the puppy and his reactions. These are the folks you want to have around your puppy. Being exposed to people other than yourself is mandatory if you want a happy dog that you can also invite to the party.

Let Your Puppy Roam

Don't lock your puppy up in another room just because you're having company. Let him roam and get comfortable with all sizes and shapes of men, women, and children. Of course, that requires your presence and attention to make sure he is behaving properly and interacting with curiosity and not fear or signs of potential aggression.

You want to start socializing with people at as early an age as possible. The sooner he realizes people are a part of his world and he knows what to expect, the happier he will be - not to mention you and your friends.

Walking Your Schnoodle Is Mandatory

Exposing your dog to people happens naturally on your daily walks. So be sure you do walk your dog minimally once a day, but more if you can.

- especially when they're young. They have energy, and they need to use it. Unwalked dogs can easily become problem dogs simply because they have too much unused energy in their body and their mind.

As a reminder, schnoodles can often be stubborn. They want to go their way, not to follow your way. Learn how to manage this tendency on your walks. Learn how to walk your dog properly with the best leash and/or harness for his tendencies. Train him to follow your lead rather than thinking he is the leader and in charge of where you're going.

Hafiz Resting After A Walk With His Next Best Friend

11

Preparing Your Friend For Being Alone

I saved this lesson for last because it is arguably the most importantfor that wonderful long-term relationship with your growing and evolving puppy. Eventually, there will come a time when you have to leave your beloved schnoodle alone. And you know this will not be aonce and done event.

Leaving your pooch on their own, without guilt or remorse, is part of being a conscientious and loving dog owner. You want to be free to truly enjoy your time out on the town or partying with friends, or when you go to your job so you can get absorbed in your work without worrying about your Schnoodle.

Most dogs naturally tend to have some separation anxiety. But your Schnoodle may have more than you realize. You can start by creating time each day for just you and your pet. No other people or animals.

Consider purchasing a baby gate and keep your little friend Gated in another room where he can be nearby but cannot follow you around wherever you go. I'm happy to report that your Schnoodle can learn to be left alone on his own for a reasonable length of time.

Hafiz Safely Hidden Away Under The Be

But dogs can get bored as well - especially intelligent ones. And both the schnauzer and poodle are well known for their smarts. So be onthe lookout for some simple signs of stress or anxiety - and respond to them with loving kindness, reassurance, and especially your attention - once again, both verbal and tactile. Here are a few of what to look for indicating anxiety is happening:

- Barking
- Panting
- Pacing
- Running In Circles
- If in an enclosed space, trying to dig their way out or climb overthe top of the enclosure

One of the best ways to start this training is to leave your puppy alone in the house for short periods of time, like 5 or 10 minutes to start. You can stand just outside the door or wait out on the street to discover which of the above things he might do.

You can increase the practice time for being alone in increments. I usedto drive around the block and listen for when my little one would finally stop barking and accept he was ok without me for a while.

If you have to leave your schnoodle alone for a whole day, arrange for a dog walker or a friend to come and take him out, even if only for 10 minutes. And if you have to go out for the evening after work, go home first and offer your friend some quality play time with lots of affection and happy expressions of joy to be with him.

Schnoodles are prone to separation anxiety. But if trained from the beginning for how to deal with it, they can learn. They trust you will return. I know some people like to leave music playing all day or have the TV on simulating the presence of humans.

I found one of the most enjoyable ways to develop that trust was cradling Hafiz in my arms, on his back, with his head so relaxed it was bobbing around a little while I gently swayed my body around like you do with a newborn, making sweet cooing sounds or singing softly directly to him.

Discover what works for you and your particular pooch. Every single dog is unique, just as is every owner.. When each learns how to meet the other's needs, you create a higher probability of everything going well, cementing that great friendship we all know can exist between owner and dog.

12

Conclusion

Well, I've shared what I found to be the most helpful in creating and maintaining a caring and loving relationship with your schnoodle that deepens and lasts over time.

Keep expanding your knowledge of what's best for your schnoodle. Read. Visit your vet. Keep up on the latest in dog nutrition and new practices for training and health.

My 15 years with Hafiz were some of the best years of my life. And as I've shared earlier, this little loving fellow gave me far more than I ever expected to get from owning a dog.

May you enjoy your little bundle of schnoodle energy and grow with him over the years. Stay open, flexible, creative, and very expressive of your love and appreciation for his presence in your life.

May you be happy, always find your way back to your center, and bask in the joy of a peaceful and heartfelt connection with another living being. It can truly change how you perceive everything.

If you found this book helpful, I'd be very appreciative if you left a favorable review for the book on Amazon.

Much love, Ragini

Hafiz Proudly Displaying His Prowess On The Park Bench

Resources

Animal Health Foundation of California. (2020, January 13). Debunking the "Alpha dog" theory.The Animal Health Foundation. https://www.animalhealthfoundation.org/blog/2020/01/debunking-the-alpha-dog- theory

Genius Vets. (2024). The good, the bad, and the truth about designed dogs. SugarRiverAnimalHospital.com. Retrieved October 10, 2024, from https://www.sugarriveranimalhospital.com/services/dogs/blg/good-bad-and-truth-about-designer-dogs

Rosling, E. (2022, April 12). 7 fun brain games for dogs mental stimulation and happiness. Barc London. https://www.barclondon. com/blogs/dog-training behaviour/brain-games-for-dogs

Schnoodle Dog: All you Need to know about care, images, and more 2024 2024. (2023, November 29). Dogfix.com. https://dogfix.com/ dog-breed/schnoodle/

Socializing your dog. (n.d.). Animal Humane Society.

https://www.ani

malhumanesociety.org/resource/socializing-your-dog

The Drake Center & The Drake Center Blog Post. (2024). Top
5 healthy dog food toppers. plymouthvet.com. Retrieved
October 10, 2024, from
https://www.plymouthvet.com/services/dogs/blog/top-5-
healthy-dog-food-toppers

Trott, S. (2024, June 20). Schnoodle: 20 Facts You Didn't
Know. SpiritDog Training.
https://spiritdogtraining.com/schnoodle-facts

We Feed Raw. (n.d.). Best 10 dog food Toppers for a healthy
pet | We feed raw. https://wefeedraw.com/blog/best-10-
healthy-dog-food- toppers

Weissinger, A. (2024, August 21). 7 best dog training treats of
2024 that'll motivate your pup. usnews.com. Retrieved
October 10, 2024, from https://www.usnews.com/360-
reviews/pets/best-dog-training- treats

About the Author

A Behavior Change Specialist and Leadership/Life Coach, Ragini Michaels has run a successful private practice for over 4 decades. She has taught around the globe, offering certification training in NLP (Neuro-Linguistic Programming), Ericksonian-Style Hypnosis, and in her original work to become a Paradox Management Consultant. For more information, please visit https://courses.RaginiMichaels.com

You can connect with me on:

https://courses.raginimichaels.com

https://www.facebook.com/ragini.e.michaels

Also by Ragini Michaels

We all want to be happy. But sometimes life gets in the way. People lose jobs. Spouses are unfaithful. Kids are hostile. Friends die. Houses burn down. It is a jungle out there. *Unflappable* is a book that helps readers not only survive but embrace these ups and downs of life and learn to stay centered and peaceful regardless of the circumstances.

Drawing on the wisdom of the mystics and her NLP (neuro-linguistic programming) training, Ms. Michaels offers a six-step process for happiness and serenity regardless of how crazy life gets.

Unflappable offers a unique route to a different brand of happiness— one that doesn't depend on outside circumstances, and incorporates a model for conscious living that leads to serenity.

Unflappable: 6 Steps To Staying Happy, Cen-tered, Peaceful No Matter What

Made in the USA
Coppell, TX
03 December 2024

40868957R00036